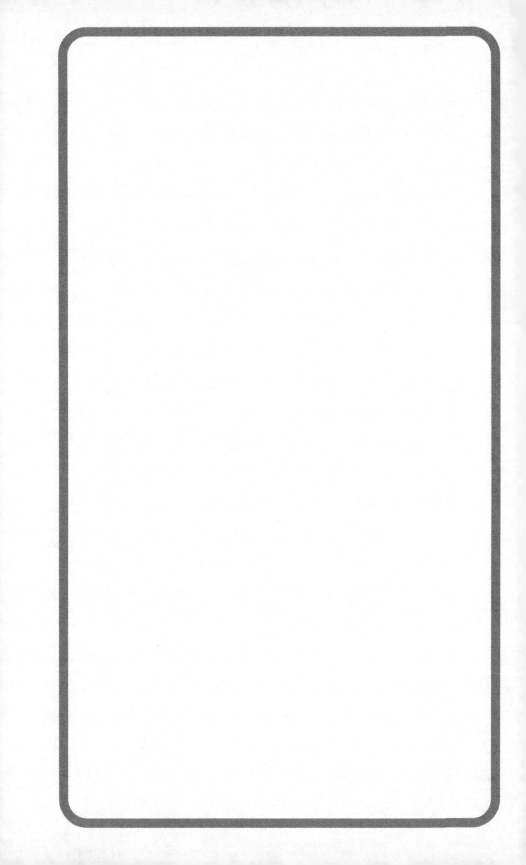

If you have any wishes or suggestions, please feel free to write us at the email address below.
If you liked the book, please let the other potential buyers know in the form of a review.
We know it takes a moment and is considered unnecessary, but you could help our small company tremendously.

Love
Maximus Designs

Legal Notice / Impressum
Copyright: Maximus Designs 2019
E-Mail: Shirtdesignerz@yahoo.com
Cover, translation and design by Maximilian Klein,Goldammerstr.18, 12351 Berlin, Germany
All rights reserved; no part of this publication may be reproduced or transmitted by any means, electronic, mechanical, photocopying or otherwise, without the prior permission of the publisher.
© 2019

Made in United States
North Haven, CT
21 June 2023

38035595R00063